# WHAT'S INSIDE?
# LINERS AND MERCHANT SHIPS

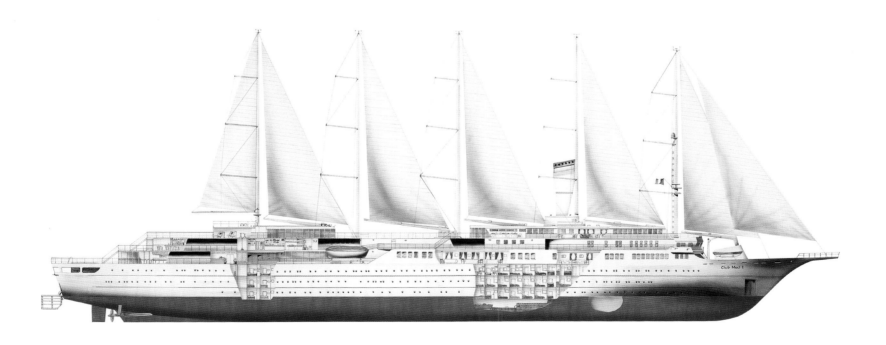

Club Med 1

# WHAT'S INSIDE?
# LINERS AND MERCHANT SHIPS

Sandy Creek
NEW YORK

An Imprint of Sterling Publishing
387 Park Avenue South
New York, NY 10016

Editorial and design by
Amber Books Ltd
74–77 White Lion Street
London N1 9PF
United Kingdom

Series Editor: Michael Spilling
Project Editor: Sarah Uttridge
Design: Brian Rust and Andrew Easton
Picture Research: Terry Forshaw

ISBN 978-1-4351-5369-1

Manufactured in China
Lot #:
2  4  6  8  10  9  7  5  3  1
09/12

# Contents

*Cutty Sark* (1869)     6

*Preussen* (1902)     10

RMS *Titanic* (1911)     14

RMS *Queen Mary* (1934)     18

*Queen Elizabeth 2* (1968)     22

CCGS *Louis S. St.-Laurent* (1969)     26

*Natchez* (1975)     30

*Berge Stahl* (1986)     34

*Wind Surf* (1990)     38

*Jervis Bay* (1992)     42

Glossary     46

Index     48

# Cutty Sark (1869)

The world's fastest sailing ships had a special name in the 19th century: clipper ships. "Clip" means to fly swiftly. British-built *Cutty Sark* was one of the fastest clippers in the world.

• • • • • • • • • • • •

*Cutty Sark* was a "China clipper," built for the long-distance trade between East Asia and the United Kingdom. Others sailed from the United States to East Asia.

## Tea Clippers

*Cutty Sark* was built in 1869 on Scotland's River Clyde, famous for its shipyards. She was termed a tea clipper because she carried tea from China, a very expensive cargo. Owners of **clipper ships** were proud of their speed and tried to set records. Clippers would race from China to England, with the winner

**The restored clipper ship *Cutty Sark* is one of London's most popular tourist attractions.**

7

A sailor on another clipper reported that *Cutty Sark* caught and passed his ship going twice as fast.

The height of the clipper ship era was from 1843 until 1869, when steamships were gaining in importance over sail. *Cutty Sark* served as a cargo vessel and later as a training ship until 1954. She is now a popular museum ship in London.

able to get to the buyers first and sell the cargo for the best price.

## Clipper Ship Museum

Clippers were narrow across the **beam**, and had extra sails for more speed. *Cutty Sark* was 212 feet (64 m) in length and could make more than 17 **knots**—or 20 miles per hour (32 km/h). She could carry 1,450 tons (1,315 metric tons) of tea.

# Did you know?

• *Cutty Sark* is named after a fictional witch who wore a short shirt—a cutty sark in Scottish. The figurehead on the bow of the ship is of this witch.

• *Cutty Sark* was damaged by fire while being restored in 2007. She reopened to the public in 2012.

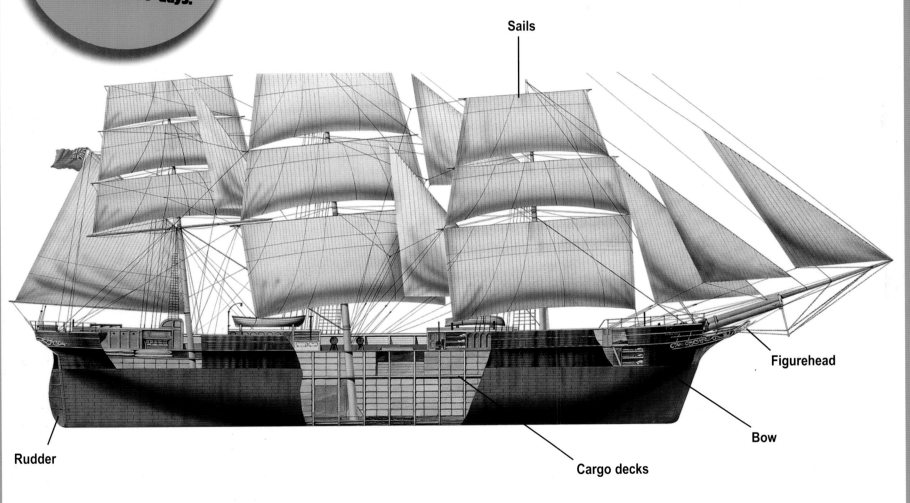

**FACT**

In 1874, *Cutty Sark* set a record time from England to Australia: 73 days.

Sails

Figurehead

Bow

Cargo decks

Rudder

# Preussen (1902)

The German state of Prussia (Preussen) had reason to be proud of a ship named in her honor in 1902. *Preussen* was one of the world's great sailing ships, a windjammer.

• • • • • • • • • • • • • • • • • •

With its many sails, steel hull, and speed, the **windjammer** was considered the "ultimate sailing ship." Windjammer refers to its sails "jamming," or holding, the wind.

## Queen of the Seas

*Preussen* was extremely sturdy because of her steel hull, and very fast because of her five masts, with six sails each. She could plow ahead through heavy storms, although eight men might be needed to hold her large steering wheel. She set a number of speed

**The German-built windjammer, *Preussen*, had 47 sails totaling 50,000 square feet (15,240 sq. m) of canvas.**

• When referring to a ship, it is incorrect to use the word the, as in: "We saw the *Preussen* this morning." Rather it should be: "We saw *Preussen* this morning."

• Windjammers sailed on very long voyages, following the routes of the ocean's prevailing winds.

records between her home port, Hamburg, in Germany, and ports in Chile. Some called her "Queen of the Seas" because of her beauty and power.

## An Early End

*Preussen* had a crew of 45. She could carry 8,900 tons (8,100 metric tons) of **bulk cargo** (such as nitrate, used in fertilizer and gunpowder). At 482

feet (147 m) long, she could reach 20 knots (23 mph; 37 km/h) under full sail with a favorable wind.

Less than ten years after her launching, *Preussen* was rammed and badly damaged by a ferry boat in the English Channel. Before she could be towed to safety, a storm struck. She was driven against rocks, and sank.

**The wreck of *Preussen*, grounded on the English coast after being accidentally rammed by a ferry boat.**

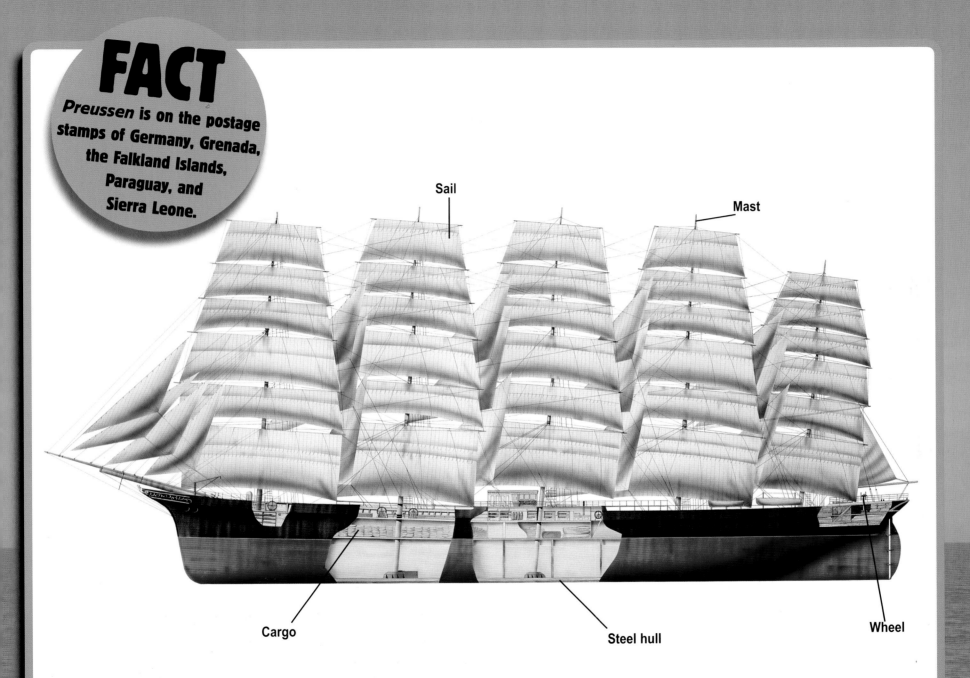

**FACT**

Preussen is on the postage stamps of Germany, Grenada, the Falkland Islands, Paraguay, and Sierra Leone.

Sail

Mast

Cargo

Steel hull

Wheel

14

# RMS Titanic (1911)

From the mid-19th century until the 1960s, most people crossed the Atlantic by ocean liner. These were ships built to carry passengers, cargo, and mail on regularly scheduled journeys between countries.

The largest, fastest, and most modern **ocean liners** traveled the North Atlantic routes between European and North American ports.

## An Unsinkable Ship

During the "golden age" of liners before World War II (1939–1945), there was fierce competition to build the best ships. In 1911, White Star Lines launched the British RMS *Titanic*, the largest, most luxurious ship ever. Many believed modern liners like *Titanic* were unsinkable. *Titanic* left Southampton, England on her **maiden voyage** for New York City on

*Titanic* **on her first and only voyage. The ship's engines were powered by steam produced by burning coal.**

April 10, 1912. On April 15, the ship hit an iceberg and sank in the North Atlantic. More than 1,500 people were lost, with 706 survivors.

**_Titanic_ sinks as survivors in lifeboats watch. The bow sank first and the stern rose into the air before the ship sank and broke apart.**

# Did you know?

• RMS stands for "Royal Mail Ship." These ships carried British mail. Because the mail had to be on time, this job was given only to the best ships.

• Ocean liners were thought unsinkable in 1912 and were not required to have enough lifeboats for everyone on board.

## _Olympic_ Class

Built in Belfast, Northern Ireland, _Titanic_ was an _Olympic_ Class ocean liner measuring 882 feet (269 m) long and 92 feet (28 m) at her widest point. When fully loaded, she weighed more than 52,000 tons (47,000 metric tons). _Titanic_ could carry 2,435 passengers and 892 crew, for a total capacity of 3,327. Her maximum speed was 24 knots (28 mph; 44 km/h). Although the crew had been warned of drifting ice, _Titanic_ was traveling at full speed when she hit the iceberg. She sank in less than three hours.

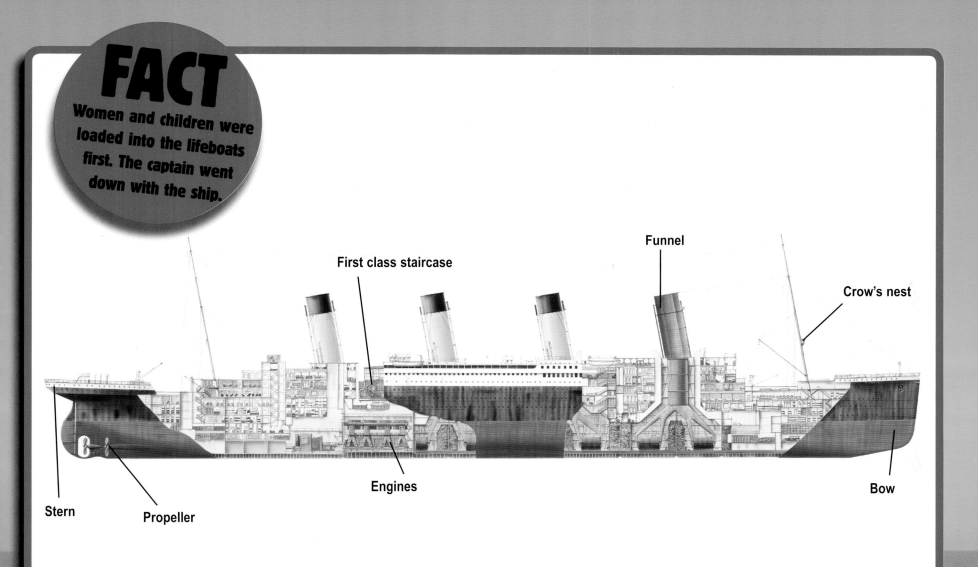

**FACT**
Women and children were loaded into the lifeboats first. The captain went down with the ship.

First class staircase

Funnel

Crow's nest

Engines

Stern

Propeller

Bow

# RMS Queen Mary (1934)

Before World War II, ocean liners were built for luxury, size, and speed. The best competed to win the prestigious Blue Riband, an award for the fastest across the Atlantic.

• • • • • • • • • • • •

Launched in 1934, **superliner** RMS *Queen Mary* won the Blue Riband in 1936 and then again in 1938. She held the record until 1952.

## Luxury Liner to Troop Ship

Through the 1930s, *Queen Mary* transported thousands of passengers across the Atlantic. With fine restaurants, libraries, and indoor swimming pools, she was one of the world's most luxurious ships. When World War II broke out, *Queen Mary* transported Allied troops. Her speed

*Queen Mary* **is now a hotel and ship museum in Long Beach, California. She is one of the few pre–World War II ocean liners still around today.**

than 30 knots (35 mph; 56 km/h). *Queen Mary* weighs over 80,000 tons (72,600 metric tons), and is more than 1,000 feet (300 m) long. She could hold 2,100 passengers and a crew of 1,100. In 1965, the liner made her 1,000th and final trip, ending in California. She became a museum and hotel.

allowed her to outrun German U-boats. In one record-setting trip, *Queen Mary* transported more than 16,000 U.S. troops to Britain. She and her sister ship, *Queen Elizabeth*, were the largest, fastest troop ships in the war.

## Royal Heritage

RMS *Queen Mary* was built in Glasgow, Scotland, and named after Mary, wife of Britain's King George V (1910–1936). Second in size only to the French liner *Normandie*, she was the fastest ship at the time, able to travel at more

# Did you know?

• During World War II, *Queen Mary* was painted navy gray. She was nicknamed the "Gray Ghost."

• British prime minister Winston Churchill crossed the Atlantic in *Queen Mary* to meet with U.S. president Franklin Roosevelt during World War II.

**FACT**
In her 30 years of service, Queen Mary carried more than 2 million passengers.

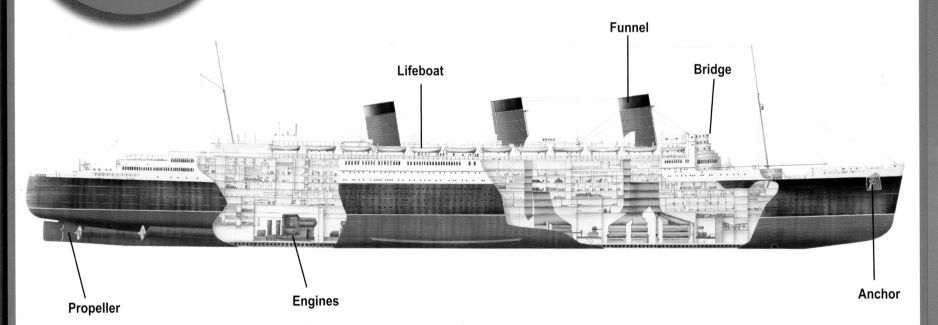

Funnel

Lifeboat

Bridge

Propeller

Engines

Anchor

# Queen Elizabeth 2 (1968)

*Queen Elizabeth 2* was one of the last great ocean liners to link Europe and America. Known as *QE2*, she was built by Cunard Line to sail from Southampton, England, to New York City.

● ● ● ● ● ● ● ● ● ● ● ● ● ● ●

QE2 was in service from 1969 to 2008, first as a **transatlantic** liner, then as a **cruise ship**. In 2008 she was sold to become a floating hotel and museum.

## Cruise Ship or Hotel?

QE2 was launched in 1968 at Scotland's Clydebank shipyards, which built several famous ships. She replaced two of them: Cunard's aging liners *Queen Mary* and *Queen Elizabeth*. Airlines were beginning to take over travel across the Atlantic, but Cunard built

**The transatlantic liner *Queen Elizabeth 2* leaves Southampton for New York in 1982. QE2 could cross the Atlantic in four days and 17 hours.**

*QE2* enters New York Harbor in 2002, passing the Statue of Liberty. She is starting out on a round-the-world cruise.

*QE2* to keep its passenger service going. She was sold in 2008 and taken to Dubai on the Persian Gulf. Her future—as a hotel or a cruise ship—is still being decided.

# Did you know?

• *QE2* is not named after Queen Elizabeth II, but after the ship, *Queen Elizabeth*.

• Queen Elizabeth II christened *QE2*. She used the same pair of gold scissors her mother (Queen Elizabeth) used to christen *Queen Elizabeth* and grandmother (Queen Mary) used for *Queen Mary*.

## Fame and Speed

Few passenger liners had the fame of *QE2*. She continued the tradition of those mighty ships steaming into New York Harbor. They carried families coming to America as well as rich and famous world travelers. *QE2* carried almost 2.5 million passengers during her 40-year career. She is the fastest merchant ship in the world, capable of reaching 34 knots (39 mph; 63 km/h). She can carry 1,777 passengers and takes a crew of 1,040. *QE2* is 963 feet (293.5 m) long and has 12 decks.

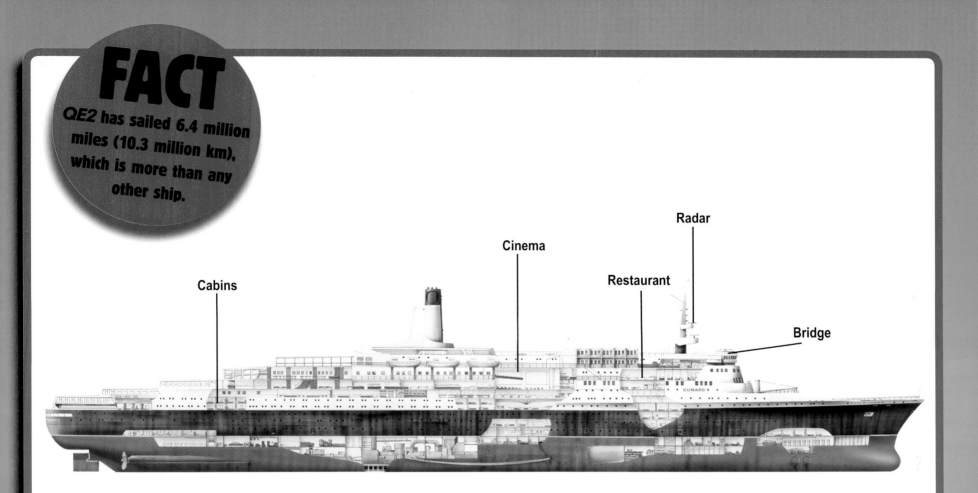

**FACT**

QE2 has sailed 6.4 million miles (10.3 million km), which is more than any other ship.

Cabins

Cinema

Restaurant

Radar

Bridge

CUNARD

**Queen Elizabeth 2 (1968)**

# CCGS Louis S. St-Laurent (1969)

Merchant vessels and tankers travel northern Canada's icy waterways, which are kept open by icebreakers. Commissioned in 1969, the Canadian Coast Guard Ship (CCGS) *Louis S. St-Laurent* is Canada's most important icebreaker.

For centuries, explorers searched for the Northwest Passage, a sea route between the Atlantic and Pacific Oceans. In 1979, *St-Laurent* broke through ice to create that passage.

## Through the Northwest Passage

On the journey to open the Northwest Passage, *St-Laurent* accompanied CCGS *Franklin*, named after 19th-century English explorer Sir John Franklin. (In 1847, Franklin died while looking for the Northwest Passage.)

**St-Laurent draws close by CCGS Healy in the Arctic Ocean in 2009.**

*St-Laurent* continued Franklin's historic journey, sailing completely around North America and back to her home port, St. John's, Newfoundland.

## Winter and Summer Duties

**Icebreaker**s serve on coastal and inland waters.

# Did you know?

• *St-Laurent*'s extremely strong bow is designed for pushing onto the ice and breaking it with the ship's weight. Sometimes an icebreaker also has to back up then ram the ice pack again and again to open it.

*St-Laurent* often operates in the Gulf of St. Lawrence to help ships sailing to and from Montreal up the St. Lawrence River. During the summer months, *St-Laurent* travels to isolated communities, bringing supplies, medicine, and needed aid. She also takes part in scientific expeditions.

Classed as a "heavy arctic icebreaker," *St-Laurent* is 393 feet (120 m) long and has a speed of 16 knots—or 18 miles per hour (30 km/h). She has a crew of 46 and carries two helicopters.

**Viewed bow on, *St-Laurent* plies the Arctic Ocean's gray and icy waters.**

**FACT**

*St-Laurent* is a "heavy Arctic icebreaker" and is the largest ship in the Canadian Coast Guard.

Bridge

Crane

Helicopter

Cabins

Coast Garde
Guard côtière

Rudder

Bow

# Natchez (1975)

*Natchez* is a sternwheel paddle steamboat on the Mississippi River. She is a reminder of the days when paddlewheel vessels ruled the waterways of the United States.

In the 19th century, grand steamboats plied American rivers, the highway system for the nation's commerce. Steamboats did not need wind and sails to move, and they could travel on almost any waterway.

## Keeping the Past in Mind

Based in New Orleans, *Natchez* carries passengers on cruises or short trips across harbors as they enjoy dinner and music. *Natchez* is a tourist vessel, but she

**Natchez passengers enjoy a harbor tour. In steamboating days, passengers stayed on the upper decks, while cargo crowded the lower parts of the vessel.**

## Built to Race

Riverboats often raced from port to port for the right to be named the fastest on the river. Today, *Natchez* regularly wins races against other riverboats.

Powered by two steam engines originally built in 1925 for the steamboat *Clairton*, *Natchez* was launched in 1975 in Louisiana. Two tall smokestacks rise high above her deck. She is made of steel, is 265 feet (81 m) long, and can enter waters as shallow as 7 feet (2 m). She weighs 1,384 tons (1,255 metric tons).

**The riverboat's powerful paddles, driven by steam engines, were symbols of progress and commerce during the 19th century.**

keeps alive the memory of **riverboats** of the past.

Steam-powered tugboats were the workhorses of river commerce, hauling towlines of **barges** filled with stone, hay, coal, and agricultural products. Paddlewheel riverboats, however, were the queens of the waterways.

## Did you know?

• While *Natchez* has her paddlewheel at the stern, or rear, sidewheeler paddlewheels are on each side of the boat.

• *Natchez* is the ninth riverboat named after the city of Natchez, Mississippi. The first was a sidewheeler, built in New York City in 1823.

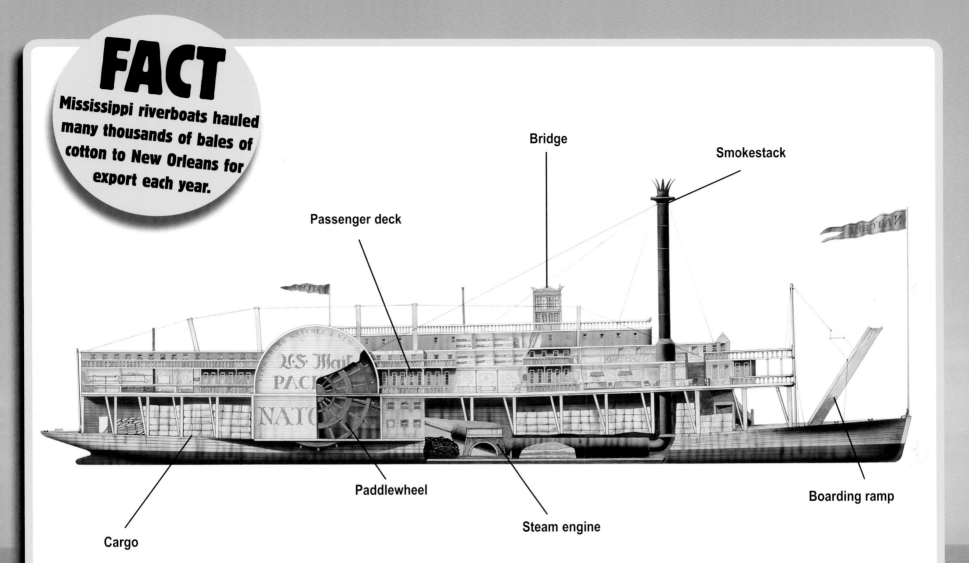

**FACT**
Mississippi riverboats hauled many thousands of bales of cotton to New Orleans for export each year.

Bridge

Smokestack

Passenger deck

Paddlewheel

Steam engine

Boarding ramp

Cargo

# Berge Stahl (1986)

Bulk carriers are vessels that transport iron ore, cement, and agricultural products such as grain. One of the world's largest bulk carriers is Norway's *Berge Stahl*.

Only two ports in the world are large and deep enough to dock *Berge Stahl* when she is fully loaded: Holland's Europort and Brazil's Ponta da Madeira.

## Iron Ore for Europe

When fully loaded, *Berge Stahl* can carry 402,086 tons (364,767 metric tons) of **iron ore**. She was built in South Korea in 1986 for a Norwegian company. At 1,122 feet (342 m) she was the longest iron ore carrier in the world until 2011. That was the year the new *Vale Brasil* entered service. *Berge Stahl* has a crew of 16 and can make 13.5

**The bulk carrier *Berge Stahl* is docked at a pier in Ponta da Madeira, Brazil. She is being loaded with iron ore for Europe.**

knots—15.5 miles per hour (25 km/h).

## Barges Finish the Journey

*Berge Stahl*'s voyage with Ponta da Madeira's iron ore takes about 14 days to reach Europort. There, cranes on the dock unload the ore onto barges. This takes three and a half

Chutes in the northwestern Australian port of Pilbara pour iron ore into *Berge Stahl*'s cargo holds.

days. Some of the most modern bulk carriers have their own equipment to load and unload themselves. Barges then ship the ore to several other ports around Europe. These barges can go through narrow canals and along rivers. Although small compared to *Berge Stahl*, these barges are also bulk carriers.

## Did you know?

• Seagoing bulk carriers make up more than 15 percent of all merchant shipping.

• South Korea is the world's leader in building the largest bulk carriers. She built *Vale Brasil* and has 18 more ships of a similar size under construction or planned.

**FACT**

*Berge Stahl's* engine has the power of more than 27,600 horses.

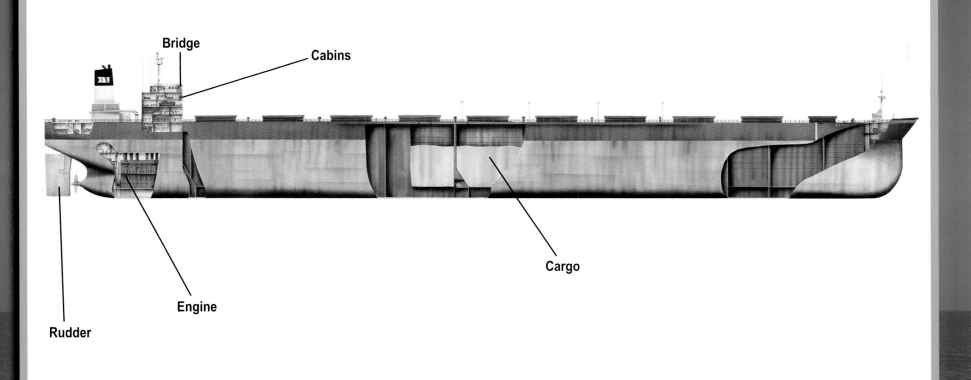

Bridge

Cabins

Cargo

Engine

Rudder

# Wind Surf (1990)

*Wind Surf* is the largest sailing ship in the world, and a luxury cruise ship for 312 tourists. She is small compared to most cruise ships, which carry several thousand passengers.

• • • • • • • • • • • • • •

*Wind Surf* offers passengers a chance to cruise while under sail. Most luxury cruise vessels are large and like floating hotels. They do not have sails.

## Computerized Sails

Launched in 1990, *Wind Surf* is owned by Windstar Cruises. She is the **flagship** in Windstar's fleet of sailing vessels. *Wind Surf* has five masts that are each 221 feet (67 m) tall, and her seven computer-operated sails **furl** and unfurl themselves. There

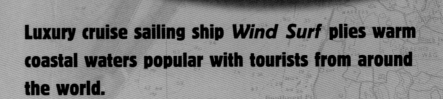

**Luxury cruise sailing ship *Wind Surf* plies warm coastal waters popular with tourists from around the world.**

## Wind and Diesel Power

*Wind Surf* can go at 12 knots (14 mph; 22 km/h) when powered by just her diesel engines. She makes 15 knots (17 mph; 27 km/h) with sails and engines working together. Her crew and staff number 191 and come from many countries. During the summer, *Wind Surf* and other Windstar vessels operate in the Mediterranean. In the winter, they sail the Caribbean as well as Costa Rica's Pacific coast. Like most cruise vessels, *Wind Surf* stops at ports where her passengers can go ashore.

**Wind Surf, with her tall masts, is well-known in Caribbean and Mediterranean tourist destinations.**

are seven decks for the passengers, who stay in 123 luxury **staterooms** with sea views. *Wind Surf* is 535 feet (162 m) in length and weighs 14,745 tons (13,376 metric tons).

## Did you know?

• *Wind Surf* has a special ballast system that keeps the ship level while in motion. This can help prevent passengers from becoming seasick.

• Cruise ship staff work 77 hours a week for 10 straight months, then have two months off.

**FACT**
The Caribbean's busiest port of call for cruise ships is Nassau, in the Bahamas.

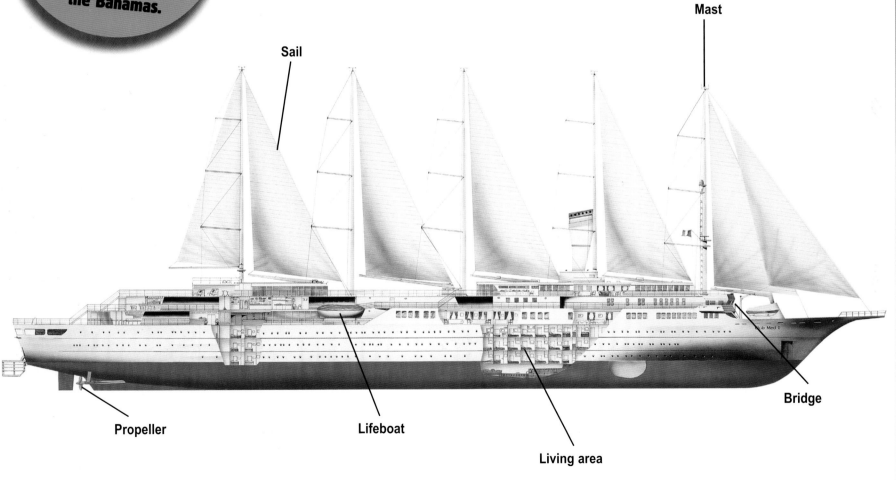

Mast

Sail

Bridge

Propeller

Lifeboat

Living area

# Jervis Bay (1992)

Built in Tokyo, Japan, in 1992, *Jervis Bay* was the first of a new class of container ships. These vessels carry cargo packed in truck-size containers measured in lengths of 20 feet (6 m).

*Jervis Bay* has room for 4,000 containers, which was a large number at the time. Now, some **container ship**s carry more than 20,000 containers.

## Container Ships

Today, most **seagoing** cargo that is factory-packaged, such as manufactured goods, is carried by container ships. The container is loaded with goods at the factory and driven by truck to the ship. Cranes load the container aboard, and unload it at

**Jervis Bay waits in port as cranes load her with containers stacked on every available space below decks and on deck.**

# Did you know?

• A container ship's cargo capacity is measured in TEUs. This means "twenty-foot equivalent units": a standard container that is 20 feet (6 m) in length.

• *Jervis Bay* is a 4,000-plus TEU container ship.

the **destination port**. Next, the container is taken by truck to the customer. Not having to load and unload individual packages of goods on and off the ship cuts on costs and time.

## Honoring Merchant Seamen

*Jervis Bay* was named after a former passenger ship that saved many merchant vessels in World War II. The HMS *Jervis Bay* was a liner taken over by the Royal Navy and armed with a few outdated guns. She was sent to protect merchant vessels from German warships. *Jervis Bay* was sunk while holding off a battleship as the merchant ships escaped. Naming a container ship *Jervis Bay* honors all those merchant seaman who risk their lives in wartime.

**With the name of previous owners, P&O Nedlloyd, on her side, *Jervis Bay* is piled high with containers.**

**FACT**
A WWII merchant seaman had a 1 in 5 chance of being killed.

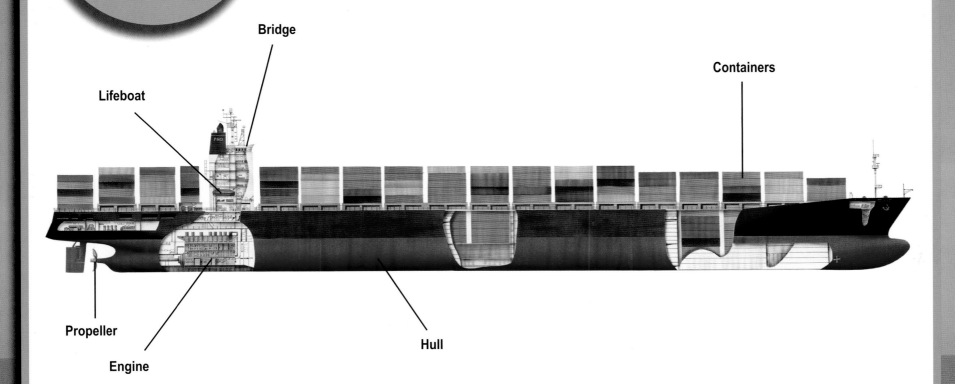

Bridge

Containers

Lifeboat

Propeller

Engine

Hull

# Glossary

**ballast**—heavy material, sometimes gravel, placed in a ship to make it more stable

**barge**—long flat-bottomed boat used to transport materials on rivers or canals

**beam**—width of a ship at its widest point

**bow**—front of a ship

**bulk cargo**—cargo that is not packaged into containers

**cargo hold**—part of the ship where the cargo is stored

**clipper ship**—fast sailing ships that were popular in the 19th century

**container ship**—ship that carries cargo in truck-size containers

**cruise ships**—passenger vessels for pleasure trips

**destination port**—port where a ship is going

**figurehead**—figure on the bow found on many sailing ships

**flagship**—ship that carries the highest-ranking officer of a fleet

**furl**—to wrap or roll up a sail

**icebreaker**—powerful ship used to break ice and open water routes so other ships can follow

**iron ore**—rocks and minerals that contain iron

**knots**—a unit of measurement used to show the speed of a ship at sea

**maiden voyage**—a ship's first voyage

**ocean liner**—ocean-going ship that carries passengers and cargo between ports on a regular schedule

**paddlewheel**—boat powered by an engine that turns a paddle wheel to push the boat through the water

**port of call**—a port where a ship stops along the way on its journey, but not its home port or destination port

**prevailing winds**—winds that blow mostly from one direction

**riverboat**—a boat built for use on rivers

**seagoing**—built for use on the ocean

**stateroom**—a private room on a ship

**stern**—back of a ship

**sternwheel**—when the paddlewheel is at the back, or stern, of a ship

**superliner**—a very large, luxurious, and fast ocean-going ship for carrying passengers

**transatlantic**—having to do with the crossing of the Atlantic Ocean

**windjammer**—a tall-masted ship with many sails

# Index

Australia 9, 36

barges 32, 36
*Berge Stahl* 34–37
Blue Riband 19
Brazil 35, 36
bulk carriers 34–37

Canada 26–29
Chile 12
China 7
Churchill, Winston 20
*Clairton,* SS 32
clippers 6–9
container ships 42–45
cotton 33
Cunard Line 23–24
*Cutty Sark* 6–9

Dubai 24

Elizabeth II, Queen 24
English Channel 12

Falkland Islands 13
France 20
*Franklin,* CCGS 27
Franklin, Sir John 27–28

George V, King 20
Germany 12, 13, 20
Grenada 13

*Healy,* CCGS 27
Holland 35

icebreakers 26–29
iron ore 35, 36

Japan 43
*Jervis Bay,* HMS 44
*Jervis Bay,* MV 42–45

lifeboats 16, 17, 21, 45
*Louis S. St-Laurent,* CCGS 26–29

Mary, Queen 20, 24
museum ships 8, 19, 20, 23

naming of ships 12, 16
*Natchez,* SS 30–33
New York City 15, 23, 24, 32
*Normandie* 20
Northwest Passage 27–28
Norway 34–37

paddlewheel ships 30–33
Paraguay 13
P&O Nedlloyd 44
Ponta da Madeira, Brazil 35, 36
*Preussen* 10–13
Prussia 11

*Queen Elizabeth,* RMS 20, 23, 24

*Queen Elizabeth 2* 22–25
*Queen Mary,* RMS 18–21, 23, 24

riverboats 30–33
Roosevelt, Franklin 20

sailing ships 6–13
Scotland 7, 20, 23
Sierra Leone 13
South Korea 35, 36
speed records 7, 11–12, 19, 32
steam ships 14–25, 30–33

tea clippers 7–8
TEUs (twenty-foot equivalent units) 44
*Titanic,* RMS 14–17
troop ships 19–20
tugboats 32

U-boats 20
United Kingdom 6–9, 14–25, 27, 42–45
United States 7, 19, 20, 24, 30–33

*Vale Brasil* 35, 36

White Star Lines 15
*Wind Surf* 38–41
windjammers 11, 12
World War II 15, 19–20, 44, 45